BOSTON COMMON PRESS
Brookline, Massachusetts

1997

Boston Common Press
17 Station Street
Brookline, Massachusetts 02147

ISBN 0-936184-17-5
Library of Congress Cataloging-in-Publication Data
The Editors of *Cook's Illustrated*
        How to make an American layer cake: An illustrated step-by-
step guide to perfect cakes, frostings, and fillings/The Editors of
Cook's Illustrated
1st ed.

        Includes 42 recipes and 41 illustrations.
        ISBN 0-936184-17-5 (hardback): $14.95
        I. Cooking. I. Title
1997

Manufactured in the United States of America

Distributed by Boston Common Press, 17 Station Street, Brookline,
MA 02147

Cover and text design by Amy Klee
Illustrations by John Burgoyne

HOW TO MAKE AN AMERICAN LAYER CAKE

THE COOK'S ILLUSTRATED LIBRARY

Illustrations by John Burgoyne

CONTENTS

introduction

I N 1938 MY MOTHER SPENT THE SUMMER near Dayton, Tennessee, at a Quaker work camp. She became friendly with two sisters, local girls, who invited her over for something to eat after work. Their home turned out to be a two-room board shack with snakes under the front porch and holes in the floorboards. Inside, their parents were dressed in their Sunday best, and sitting on the kitchen table was a large white cake.

It was a poor county, the Depression was still very much in evidence, and the cake was a kind gesture indeed, a way of greeting a special visitor. My mother was handed a large piece of cake, and as she bit into it, she noticed it was covered with small red ants. Of course, she ate the whole piece, but years later, when she first told me this story, I recall how special that cake was for her, ants and all. A layer cake is a truly American way of saying hello, happy birthday, congratulations, or welcome home. Baking a cake says as much about the cook as it does the guest.

These days, cake making has become something of a dying art. Too many home cooks rely on boxed mixes, which are not much less work than a good from-scratch recipe, or cakes purchased at local stores. But nothing matches the joy and taste of a good homemade layer cake. It is an honest, forthright expression of the American kitchen, a delicious celebration of simple ingredients with universal appeal.

The sheer practicality of a layer cake recipe makes it a worthy subject for a small cookbook such as this. Once the basics of a yellow, white, and chocolate cake are mastered, the home cook can easily go on to many variations. A yellow cake is the basis for a score of recipes from spice cake to lemon cake. A basic white cake, with a change of frosting, is turned into a coconut cake. A simple chocolate cake becomes a devil's food or German chocolate cake.

We have also published *How to Make a Pie,* and many other titles will soon be available in this series. To order other books, call us at 800-611-0759. We are also the editors and publishers of *Cook's Illustrated,* a bimonthly publication about American home cooking.

Christopher P. Kimball
Publisher and Editor
Cook's Illustrated

chapter one

CAKE BASICS

THE RECIPES IN THIS BOOK WILL teach you how to make a variety of classic American layer cakes. There are some rules to bear in mind as you work through the recipes. Follow this checklist for success every time.

CHECK YOUR OVEN TEMPERATURE WITH AN OVEN THERMOMETER. If your oven is too hot, the sides of the cake will set before the middle does, and the cake will hump or crack. If your oven is too cold, the air will escape from the batter before the batter begins to set, and the cake will have a coarse texture and may even fall.

▪▪ **USE ROUND CAKE PANS THAT MEASURE EITHER EIGHT OR NINE INCHES ACROSS.** Some recipes call for eight-inch cake pans, others for nine-inch pans. Use the correct size. If the pans are too large, they overheat the rim of the cake, causing the same sorts of problems as an overheated oven. If the pans are too small, batter may rise right out of them. Choose sturdy aluminum pans with absolutely vertical sides. Do not use disposable foil pans.

▪▪ **GENEROUSLY GREASE THE PANS WITH SHORTENING—NOT BUTTER—AND COAT THEM WELL WITH FLOUR.** Butter contains water, which when it evaporates may leave greaseless gaps to which cake batter can stick. Solid vegetable shortening, such as Crisco, is 100 percent fat and won't leave gaps. The flour holds the shortening in place and keeps the batter from seeping through to the pan bottom. We find that shiny cake pans are almost nonstick, so there is no need for parchment paper liners. If you are using an older pan with a dull finish, as an extra precaution you may want to grease the pan, line the bottom with a piece of parchment or waxed paper, grease the paper, and then flour the pan and paper.

▪▪ **HAVE ALL INGREDIENTS, ESPECIALLY BUTTER, EGGS, AND MILK, AT ROOM TEMPERATURE.** Chilled ingredients do not emulsify well, which leads to a dense cake, and cold butter won't even mix into a batter. Very warm ingredients may cause air cells in creamed butter to dissolve. All ingredients should register between 65 and 70 degrees on an instant-read thermometer. Let butter soften on the counter for about an hour before creaming. The sticks should give when pressed, but still hold their shape with no signs of melting.

MEASURE FLOUR CAREFULLY BY THE DIP-AND-SWEEP METHOD. Dip the measuring cup into the container of flour, scoop out a heaping cupful, and then level the top with the straight edge on a butter knife or icing spatula. Do not shake, tap, or pack the cup. If the cup is not completely filled on the first try, dump the flour back into the container and dip again. For guaranteed accuracy, measure the flour by weight following the dip-and-sweep. For our recipes, measure the flour before sifting. This is essential because sifted flour weighs far less than unsifted. Use a cake sifter to remove any lumps from flour (or confectioners' sugar) and aerate dry ingredients.

USE FRESH BAKING POWDER. As soon as a can of baking powder is opened, the acid and alkali components start to react. Within a few months, baking powder will lose some strength. When opening a can, write the date on the bottom and discard the baking powder after three months.

⣿ DIVIDE BATTER EVENLY BETWEEN PANS. Cake layers of different heights can pose a problem when it comes time to frost and decorate. Use a scale to make sure that equal amouints of batter go into each pan (*see* figure 1).

Figure 1.
To ensure that you end up with equal amounts of batter in each cake pan, use a kitchen scale to measure the weight of each filled pan.

11

▪▪ INSULATE THE PANS TO ENSURE EVEN COOKING.
By providing a buffer between the sides of a cake pan and
the oven heat, Magi-Cake Strips or damp newspaper prevent overcooking near the outside edges. The result is a level
cake that does not shrink or crack and does not have a
tough outer crust (*see* figures 2-4).

Figure 2.
Saturate each Magi–Cake
Strip with cold water.
Run your fingers
along it to squeeze out
excess water.

12

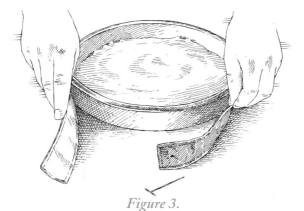

Figure 3.

*With the aluminized side facing out, wrap the strip around the out-
side of the batter-filled pan. Secure the strip with the provided pin.
Bake as directed, but note that cooking times may increase slightly.*

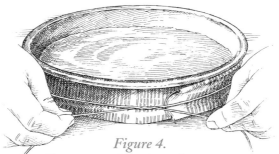

Figure 4.

*Newspaper can be used to make your own
Magi-Cake Strips. Fold a sheet of newspaper to make a strip
the width of the pan height. Wet the strip and wrap it around
the cake pan. Secure the strip with wet kitchen twine.*

13

⁙ GIVE PANS ENOUGH SPACE IN THE OVEN. Cakes placed too close to one another will rise toward each other and end up lopsided. Cakes placed too close to the oven walls won't rise as high on the side nearest the wall. Keep pans at least three inches from each other and the oven walls and on the middle rack of the oven. If your oven is small, stagger the pans on racks set at the upper-middle and lower-middle positions to allow for proper air circulation.

⁙ USE YOUR FINGER AND A CAKE TESTER TO JUDGE WHEN LAYERS ARE DONE. Layer cakes should be baked until firm in the center when lightly pressed and a cake needle or toothpick inserted in the center comes out clean or with just a crumb or two adhering.

⁙ COOL CAKE LAYERS IN THEIR PANS, THEN ON RACKS. Grease racks with nonstick vegetable spray to keep cake layers from sticking to them. Do not frost the layers until they are completely cooled. Cake layers are best frosted the day they are made. However, layers may be wrapped tightly in plastic and stored at room temperature for a day. For longer storage, freeze wrapped layers for up to one month. Defrost them on the counter and unwrap them just before frosting.

▪▪ **FROST THE CAKE TWICE.** We prefer to apply a thin base coat of frosting to seal in the crumbs. We then refrigerate the cake until the frosting is set and add a thicker second coat of frosting (*see* figures 5-11).

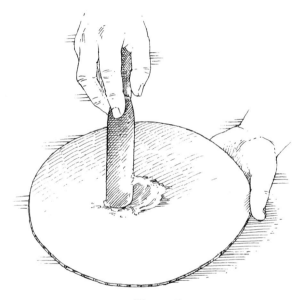

Figure 5.

To frost a standard two-layer cake, place on the cake stand a cardboard round cut to a slightly smaller diameter than the layers. Dab a little frosting in the center of the round to anchor the cake in place. You may place the dab of frosting directly on the cake plate if desired.

Figure 6.
Center one cake layer, bottom side up, on the cardboard round
(or cake plate). Place a large blob of frosting in the center of the layer.
Use a long frosting spatula to spread the icing without lifting up.

Figure 7.
Hold the edge of the spatula at a 45-degree angle against the
top of the frosted layer. Gently turn the cake stand to remove the
excess frosting and level it off.

16

Figure 8.
Place the unfrosted layer, bottom side up, on a greased tart pan
bottom and slide it onto the frosted bottom layer, making sure
that the layers are aligned.

Figure 9.
Apply a thin basecoat of frosting to seal in the crumbs.
Start by using the icing spatula to place a big dab of frosting
on the side of the cake. Move the spatula down against the
side of the cake to spread out the frosting. Repeat the process
until the side is covered.

18

Figure 10.
Lightly frost the top of the cake in the same manner as the first
layer. Refrigerate the cake until the frosting is set, about 10 minutes.

Figure 11.
Apply a thick final layer of frosting to the top and sides of the cake.

19

chapter two

YELLOW LAYER CAKES

THERE ARE TWO BASIC METHODS for making a yellow cake. The 1-2-3-4 cake dates back to the nineteenth century. The name refers to the ingredients (1 cup butter, 2 cups sugar, 3 cups flour, and 4 eggs). The recipe was easy to remember and helpful for cooks who did not have standardized measures because they could use the same cup to measure all the ingredients.

This cake is made by creaming the butter and sugar until light and fluffy. The eggs are beaten in, and then the dry ingredients are added alternately with milk or another liquid (orange juice for an orange layer cake, for instance). A second

20

kind of yellow cake is made by creaming the flour with the butter and sugar. The eggs and liquid ingredients are then added. Beating the flour with the butter coats it with fat and slows down the absorption of liquid. This method inhibits the formation of gluten, the elastic proteins that give bread and other baked goods their structure.

We made cakes with both methods and prefer the traditional creaming of butter and sugar without the flour, as in the 1-2-3-4 cake. A good butter cake should have enough chew and heft to stand up to almost any frosting. We found that yellow cakes made by creaming the flour with the butter and sugar have an overly fine grain and fragile crumb.

Bleached all-purpose flour delivers the best balance of softness and structure in our version of the 1-2-3-4 cake, which contains less flour than the original. Cake flour does not have enough protein and makes an overly soft cake. Unbleached all-purpose has too much protein and makes a tougher cake.

Traditional recipes for the 1-2-3-4 cake often call for separated eggs. The yolks are beaten into the batter after the butter and sugar are creamed while the whites are whipped to stiff peaks and folded in after the flour and milk are incorporated. Although the separated-egg method makes an especially light cake, our tests revealed it can lead to tunneling and air pockets. We had more reliable results (and no tunneling) when we added whole eggs to the batter.

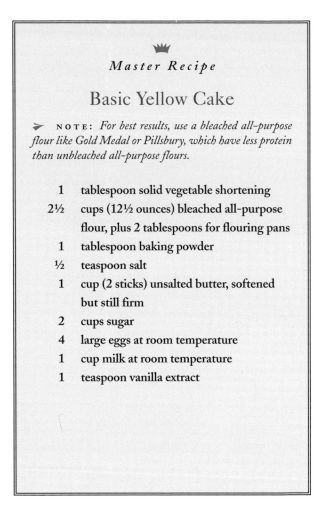

Master Recipe

Basic Yellow Cake

➤ **NOTE:** *For best results, use a bleached all-purpose flour like Gold Medal or Pillsbury, which have less protein than unbleached all-purpose flours.*

1	tablespoon solid vegetable shortening
2½	cups (12½ ounces) bleached all-purpose flour, plus 2 tablespoons for flouring pans
1	tablespoon baking powder
½	teaspoon salt
1	cup (2 sticks) unsalted butter, softened but still firm
2	cups sugar
4	large eggs at room temperature
1	cup milk at room temperature
1	teaspoon vanilla extract

♛

Master Instructions

1. Set oven rack in middle position. (If oven is too small to hold both layers comfortably on a single rack, set racks in upper-middle and lower-middle positions.) Heat oven to 350 degrees. Coat bottom and sides of two 9-inch-by-1½-inch or -2-inch round cake pans with ½ tablespoon shortening each. Sprinkle 1 tablespoon flour into each pan; roll pans in all directions to coat. Invert pans and rap sharply to remove excess flour.

2. Sift together remaining flour, baking powder, and salt. Set dry ingredients aside.

3. Beat butter in bowl of electric mixer at medium speed until smooth, about 30 seconds. Add sugar and beat, scraping down sides of bowl as needed, until light and fluffy, 2 to 3 minutes. Add eggs, one at a time, beating well after each addition. Stop mixer and scrape down sides of bowl as needed.

4. Combine milk and vanilla. With mixer on low, add some of dry ingredients *(continued on next page)*

★

Master Instructions
Basic Yellow Cake

4. *(continued from previous page)* followed by a little of milk mixture. Continue alternating dry with liquid ingredients, ending with dry ingredients. Scrape down sides of bowl as needed throughout mixing process.

5. Divide batter evenly between two prepared cake pans; using rubber spatula, spread batter to pan walls and smooth tops. Arrange pans at least 3 inches from oven walls and 3 inches apart. (If oven is too small, place pans on separate racks in staggered fashion to allow for air circulation.) Bake until firm in center when lightly pressed and cake needle or toothpick inserted in center comes out clean or with just a crumb or two adhering, 30 to 35 minutes.

6. Cool cakes in pans set on rack for 5 minutes. Loosen from sides of pans with knife, if necessary, and invert onto greased cake racks. Reinvert onto additional greased racks. Let cool completely, about 1 hour.

Classic Yellow Layer Cake with Chocolate Buttercream

➤ **NOTE:** *This is our version of America's favorite layer cake with buttery yellow cake layers and rich, creamy chocolate frosting. These yellow cake layers can be frosted with any of the buttercreams or decorating frostings in chapter 5. Coffee Buttercream is an especially good choice.*

1   recipe Basic Yellow Cake (*see* page 22)
1   recipe Chocolate Buttercream (*see* page 68)

INSTRUCTIONS:

1. Prepare cake and frosting.

2. When layers are cool, frost cake.

Old-Fashioned Strawberry Layer Cake with Whipped Cream Frosting

➤ **N O T E :** *To enhance the flavor in out-of-season berries, sprinkle the fruit sliced for the in-between layer (step 2) with one teaspoon of sugar and let it stand for fifteen minutes.*

1   recipe Basic Yellow Cake (*see* page 22)
1   recipe Whipped Cream Frosting (*see* page 83)
1   quart (19 ounces) medium-sized strawberries, lightly rinsed, thoroughly dried, and hulled

I N S T R U C T I O N S :

1. Prepare and cool cake layers. Prepare frosting.

2. Cut three-quarters of strawberries in half through stem ends.

3. Place first cake layer on cardboard round or cake plate. Frost top with ¼-inch-thick layer of whipped cream. Lay halved strawberries, cut side down, over whipped cream in single layer. Fill in spaces between berries with a little more whipped cream.

4. Add second cake layer. Press down lightly to secure. Frost top and sides of cake. Arrange remaining whole strawberries, stem side down, in decorative fashion on top of cake.

Orange Layer Cake

➤ **N O T E :** *Three medium oranges will yield enough zest and juice for the cake layers.*

1 **recipe Basic Yellow Cake (*see* page 22), with changes below**
1 **recipe Orange Buttercream (*see* page 68) or Orange Decorating Frosting (*see* page 74)**

I N S T R U C T I O N S :

1. Follow master recipe for Basic Yellow Cake, adding 1 tablespoon grated orange zest after last egg and replacing milk with 1 cup orange juice at room temperature.

2. When layers are cool, frost cake.

Almond Layer Cake

➤ **NOTE:** *Almond extract gives the cake layers a subtle almond flavor. Lightly toast the chopped almonds for the garnish in a 350-degree oven for eight minutes to bring out their flavor. See figure 12 for information on how to press the almonds or other nuts into the sides of a cake.*

1 recipe Basic Yellow Cake (*see* page 22),
  with changes below
1 recipe Almond Buttercream (*see* page 68)
  or Almond Decorating Frosting (*see* page 74)
1 cup chopped almonds, lightly toasted

INSTRUCTIONS:

1. Follow master recipe for Basic Yellow Cake, adding 1 teaspoon almond extract along with vanilla extract to milk.

2. When layers are cool, frost cake. Press almonds into sides of cake with bench scraper.

Figure 12
To coat the sides of the frosted cake with chopped or sliced nuts,
use a bench scraper or a wide, flat spatula to lift some nuts onto
the sides of the cake. Lightly toasting the nuts brings
out their flavor. Plan on using 1 cup to decorate the sides
of a standard two-layer cake.

Lemon Layer Cake

➤ **NOTE:** *In order to get a strong lemon flavor, use lemon extract (made from the oils in the yellow peel) in the cake batter. Lemon juice is too weak and can curdle the milk.*

> 1   **recipe Basic Yellow Cake (***see* **page 22), with changes below**
> 1   **recipe Lemon Buttercream (***see* **page 68) or Lemon Decorating Frosting (***see* **page 74)**

▪▪ **INSTRUCTIONS:**

1. Follow master recipe for Basic Yellow Cake, adding 1 tablespoon grated lemon zest and 1½ teaspoons lemon extract after last egg.

2. When layers are cool, frost cake.

▪▪ **VARIATIONS:**

For Lemon Layer Cake with Lemon Curd Filling and Vanilla Frosting, cover bottom layer with Lemon Curd Filling (*see* page 85) and use Vanilla Buttercream (*see* page 66) or Vanilla Decorating Frosting (*see* page 72) to cover sides and top of cake.

Spice Layer Cake
with Meringue Frosting

➤ **NOTE:** *The sweet meringue frosting complements the spices in the cake layers without overpowering them. The flavor of the spices intensifies after a day, so you may want to make the layers one day and frost them the next.*

1   **recipe Basic Yellow Cake (*see* page 22),**
    with changes below
1   **recipe Meringue Frosting (*see* page 80)**

⁞ INSTRUCTIONS:

1. Follow master recipe for Basic Yellow Cake, sifting 1½ teaspoons ground cinnamon and ½ teaspoon each ground ginger, freshly grated nutmeg, and ground cloves with flour and other dry ingredients.

2. When layers are cool, frost cake.

Country Buttermilk Layer Cake with Maple Meringue Frosting

➤ **N O T E :** *The lactic acid in the buttermilk makes a rich cake with a slightly coarser crumb. It also highlights the butter flavor. The maple frosting is reminiscent of old farm cakes from New England.*

| 1 | recipe Basic Yellow Cake (*see* page 22), with changes below |
| 1 | recipe Maple Meringue Frosting (*see* page 81) |

I N S T R U C T I O N S :

1. Follow master recipe for Basic Yellow Cake, sifting ¼ teaspoon baking soda with other dry ingredients and replacing milk with 1 cup buttermilk at room temperature.

2. When layers are cool, frost cake.

Marble Layer Cake
with Chocolate Frosting

➤ **NOTE**: *A little melted semisweet chocolate is beaten into half the batter. The two batters are then spooned into the cake pans and swirled with a butter knife. Melt the chocolate in a microwave (set at 50 percent power, stirring every minute or so until smooth) or a double boiler.*

    1   **recipe Basic Yellow Cake (***see* **page 22),
           with changes below**

    1   **recipe Chocolate Buttercream (***see* **page 68)
           or Chocolate Decorating Frosting (***see* **page 74)**

▓ INSTRUCTIONS:

1. Follow master recipe for Basic Yellow Cake, making the following changes: Equally divide batter between two bowls. Stir 1½ ounces melted and cooled semisweet chocolate into one bowl and mix well. Drop several spoonfuls of yellow batter in various spots around one prepared cake pan. Drop several spoonfuls of chocolate batter in different places in same pan. Repeat until half of each batter has been used. Being careful not to touch bottom or sides of pan, gently draw butter knife through batters to create swirls. Smooth out batter. Repeat with remaining batter in second pan.

2. When layers are cool, frost cake.

chapter three

3

WHITE
LAYER CAKES

WHITE CAKES ARE THE CLASSIC choice for birthdays. A white cake is simply a yellow butter cake made with egg whites instead of whole eggs. The whites produce the characteristic color and also make the cake soft and fine-grained. Some white cakes can be a bit dry (the missing yolks provide richness to yellow cakes) and cottony. Many white cakes also are riddled with small holes.

These problems often result when white cakes are mixed by the same method as yellow cakes, that is, the butter and sugar are creamed, and the dry ingredients are added alternately with milk. (Most white cake recipes call for stiffly beaten egg whites, which are folded in at the end.) This method exposes the flour directly to the liquid and leads to gluten formation. Although a little gluten formation is fine in a sturdier yellow cake, in a white cake (made without tenderizing yolks) the texture becomes tough. In addition, the gluten forms a stretchy net of ropelike fibers that press the air cells in the beaten whites into holes and tunnels.

To prevent overglutenization in white cake batter, we prefer to cream the flour with the butter and sugar. Because the flour is mixed with the butter at the start, it is partially waterproofed and thus less prone to gluten development. This mixing method helps keep the crumb soft and delicate.

Our kitchen tests demonstrated that beaten egg whites are responsible for the formation of air pockets. Contrary to popular wisdom, beating the whites does not produce an ethereal texture. In fact, beating causes protein strands in the whites to uncoil and link up. These clumps of egg whites cannot be incorporated into the batter and cause unsightly holes when the cake is baked.

We found that unbeaten whites mix easily into the batter when added along with the milk. They set and stiffen in the oven to provide the structure necessary to hold the fine air bubbles beaten into the butter when it is creamed. The result is a velvety cake with a delicate texture, high rise, and delicious flavor.

Master Recipe

Basic White Cake

➤ N O T E : *Low-protein cake flour makes these layers especially tender with a fine, delicate crumb. If you have forgotten to bring the milk and egg whites to room temperature, combine as directed in step 2 and then set the bottom of the glass measuring cup in a sink of hot water and stir until the mixture feels cool rather than cold, about 70 degrees.*

2	tablespoons solid vegetable shortening
2	heaping tablespoons all-purpose flour for flouring pans
1	cup milk at room temperature
¾	cup egg whites (about 6 large or 5 extra large) at room temperature
2	teaspoons vanilla extract
2¼	cups (10⅛ ounces) plain cake flour
1¾	cups sugar
4	teaspoons baking powder
1	teaspoon salt
¾	cup (1½ sticks) unsalted butter, softened but still firm

♛

Master Instructions

1. Set oven rack in middle position. (If oven is too small to hold both layers comfortably on a single rack, set racks in upper-middle and lower-middle positions.) Heat oven to 350 degrees. Coat bottom and sides of two 9-inch-by-1½-inch or -2-inch round cake pans with 1 tablespoon shortening each. Sprinkle 1 heaping tablespoon flour into each pan; roll pans in all directions to coat. Invert pans and rap sharply to remove excess flour.

2. Pour milk, egg whites, and vanilla into 2-cup measure and mix with fork until blended.

3. Mix cake flour, sugar, baking powder, and salt in bowl of electric mixer at low speed until combined. Add butter; continue beating at low speed until mixture resembles coarse crumbs, 2 to 3 minutes.

4. Add all but ½ cup of milk mixture to crumbs and beat at medium speed (or high if using handheld mixer) for 1½ minutes. Add remaining ½ cup of milk mixture and beat 30 seconds. *(continued on next page)*

Master Instructions
Basic White Cake

4. *(continued from previous page)* Stop mixer and scrape down sides of bowl. Return mixer to medium (or high) speed and beat 20 seconds longer.

5. Divide batter evenly between two prepared cake pans; using rubber spatula, spread batter to pan walls and smooth tops. Arrange pans at least 3 inches from oven walls and 3 inches apart. (If oven is too small, place pans on separate racks in staggered fashion to allow for air circulation.) Bake until firm in center when lightly pressed and cake needle or toothpick inserted in center comes out clean or with just a crumb or two adhering, 23 to 25 minutes.

6. Cool cakes in pans set on rack for 3 minutes. Loosen from sides of pans with knife, if necessary, and invert onto greased cake racks. Reinvert onto additional greased racks. Let cool completely, about 1 hour.

Classic White Layer Cake with Vanilla Frosting and Raspberry-Almond Filling

➤ **N O T E :** *This all-purpose birthday cake is delicate and light. Chopped almonds, which have first been lightly toasted in a 350-degree oven for six minutes, are folded into the vanilla frosting that covers the bottom layer. A thin layer of raspberry jam is then spread over this frosting. If you decide not to decorate with a pastry bag, use Vanilla Buttercream (see page 66) instead of the firmer decorating frosting. In either case, see figures 13–15 for information on how to write a special message on top of the cake.*

1	recipe **Basic White Cake** (*see* page 36), with changes below
½	cup blanched slivered almonds, toasted and chopped coarse
1	recipe **Vanilla Decorating Frosting** (*see* page 72)
⅓	cup seedless raspberry jam

▓ I N S T R U C T I O N S :

1. Follow master recipe for Basic White Cake, adding 2 teaspoons almond extract along with 1 teaspoon vanilla.

2. When layers are cool, combine almonds with ½ cup frosting in small bowl. Use this mixture to cover top of bottom layer. Refrigerate several minutes to set frosting.

3. Carefully spread jam over frosting. Add second layer and frost top and sides of cake with remaining plain frosting.

❖ VARIATION:

For Classic White Layer Cake with Vanilla Frosting and Lemon Curd Filling, make Basic White Cake without almond extract. Omit almonds but still coat top of bottom layer with a little plain frosting and refrigerate until set. Carefully spread ½ cup Lemon Curd Filling (*see* page 85) instead of raspberry jam over frosting. Add second layer and frost top and sides of cake.

Figure 13.
When writing "Happy Birthday" or something else on a cake,
thin the icing with a few drops of water or extract to
make it flow more smoothly. Write your message (in block or
cursive writing) with a pen or pencil on a piece of paper.
Tape the paper to a flat surface and cover it with a sheet of clear
acetate or plastic. Practice going over the message several times.
Keep wiping the icing away and trying again until you are
confident. When making printed letters, hold the bag vertically.
When making cursive letters, tilt the bag a little as you write.

41

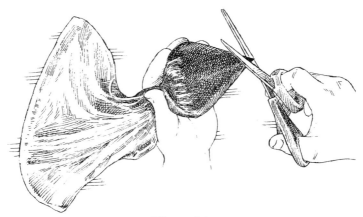

Figure 14.
Melted chocolate can also be used to decorate cakes or to write
messages. Put the chocolate in a heat-safe zipper-lock plastic bag
and immerse it in simmering water until the chocolate melts.
Snip off the very tip of one corner of the bag.

Figure 15.
Holding the bag in one hand, gently squeeze the chocolate out of
the bag. Discard the bag when finished.

43

Southern Coconut Layer Cake

➤ NOTE: *For this southern classic, cover white cake layers with billowy, soft meringue and then sprinkle generously with sweetened flaked coconut.*

   1   **recipe Basic White Cake (*see* page 36)**
   1   **recipe Meringue Frosting (*see* page 80)**
   2   **cups lightly packed sweetened flaked coconut**

■ INSTRUCTIONS:

1. Prepare and cool cake layers. Prepare frosting.

2. Frost cake. Sprinkle top of cake with coconut and press remaining coconut into sides of cake.

Walnut Layer Cake
with Maple Meringue Frosting

➤ **NOTE**: *Make sure the nuts are finely chopped by hand or in the food processor and then lightly toasted in a 350-degree oven for eight minutes. Cool the nuts before adding them to the batter.*

1   recipe Basic White Cake (*see* page 36),
     with changes below
1   recipe Maple Meringue Frosting (*see* page 81)

⁞ INSTRUCTIONS:

1. Follow master recipe for Basic White Cake, folding in ¾ cup finely chopped and lightly toasted walnuts when finished beating batter.

2. When layers are cool, frost cake.

⁞ VARIATION:

For Almond Layer Cake with Maple Meringue Frosting, add 2 teaspoons almond extract to Basic White Cake along with 1 teaspoon vanilla. Fold in ¾ cup finely chopped and lightly toasted whole almonds instead of walnuts.

chapter four

ₑ

CHOCOLATE LAYER CAKES

HOCOLATE CAKES CAN BE LIGHT AND tender, rich and fudgy, or anywhere in between. Minor ingredient changes may produce significant differences in texture and flavor. A master recipe with five variations follows. Each variation is quite distinct and is matched with a frosting that complements the cake layers.

There are a number of general principles that apply to all chocolate cakes. The most important issue is the chocolate. We have found that dissolving cocoa in boiling water produces the best chocolate cake. The color is dark and the chocolate flavor intense. Mixing cocoa into the batter with the dry ingredients does not yield the same strong flavor or dark color.

Our kitchen tests show that cakes made with unsweetened or semisweet chocolate, as opposed to cocoa powder, are not as moist or flavorful. Cooking the chocolate over boiling water for several minutes ruptures some of the cocoa particles and helps release more flavor. But in the end, cocoa powder is more easily incorporated in cake batters and delivers more punch.

Nonalkalinized natural cocoas like Hershey's make a cake that is slightly blacker and pleasantly bitter. Cakes made with dutched cocoa, which has been treated with an alkali to raise its pH, tend to have a fainter, mellower chocolate flavor. The distinctions are minor, but we prefer natural American cocoa in the following recipes.

The liquid ingredients in a chocolate cake are the other important variable. Milk (as opposed to water) mutes the chocolate flavor (dairy fat is a flavor blocker) but also makes the texture a little more substantial. Buttermilk and yogurt tenderize the crumb and add moistness while sour cream results in a dense yet melting texture.

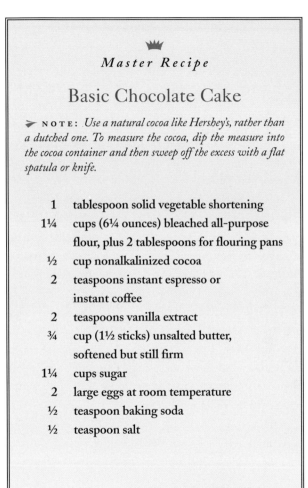

Master Recipe

Basic Chocolate Cake

➤ **NOTE:** *Use a natural cocoa like Hershey's, rather than a dutched one. To measure the cocoa, dip the measure into the cocoa container and then sweep off the excess with a flat spatula or knife.*

1	tablespoon solid vegetable shortening
1¼	cups (6¼ ounces) bleached all-purpose flour, plus 2 tablespoons for flouring pans
½	cup nonalkalinized cocoa
2	teaspoons instant espresso or instant coffee
2	teaspoons vanilla extract
¾	cup (1½ sticks) unsalted butter, softened but still firm
1¼	cups sugar
2	large eggs at room temperature
½	teaspoon baking soda
½	teaspoon salt

♛
Master Instructions

1. Set oven rack in middle position. Heat oven to 350 degrees. Coat bottom and sides of two 8-inch-by-1½-inch or -2-inch round cake pans with ½ tablespoon shortening each. Sprinkle 1 tablespoon flour into each pan; roll pans in all directions to coat. Invert pans and rap sharply to remove excess flour.

2. Mix cocoa and espresso or coffee in small bowl; add 1 cup boiling water and mix until smooth. Cool to room temperature, then stir in vanilla; set aside.

3. Beat butter in bowl of electric mixer at medium-high speed until smooth, about 30 seconds. Gradually sprinkle in sugar; beat until mixture is fluffy and almost white, 3 to 5 minutes. Add eggs, one at a time, beating 1 full minute after each addition. Stop mixer and scrape down sides of bowl as needed.

4. Whisk remaining flour, baking soda, and salt in medium bowl. With mixer on lowest speed, add one-third of dry ingredients, followed immediately by one-third of cocoa mixture; *(continued on next page)*

Master Instructions
Basic Chocolate Cake

4. *(continued from previous page)* mix until ingredients are almost incorporated into batter. Repeat process twice more. When batter appears blended, stop mixer and scrape down sides of bowl. Return mixer to low speed; beat until batter looks satiny, about 15 seconds.

5. Divide batter evenly between two prepared cake pans; using rubber spatula, spread batter to pan walls and smooth tops. Arrange pans at least 3 inches from oven walls and 3 inches apart. (If oven is too small, place pans on separate racks in staggered fashion to allow for air circulation.) Bake until firm in center when lightly pressed and cake needle or toothpick inserted in center comes out clean or with just a crumb or two adhering, 23 to 30 minutes.

6. Cool cakes in pans set on rack for 10 minutes. Loosen from sides of pans with knife, if necessary, and invert onto greased cake racks. Reinvert onto additional greased racks. Let cool completely, about 1 hour.

Velvet Devil's Food Layer Cake with Coffee Buttercream

➤ **NOTE:** *The texture of this cake is both soft and dense, similar to a chocolate pound cake, only softer and lighter. The flavor is intensely chocolate, yet pleasantly sweet. The rich coffee buttercream stands up to the dense texture of the cake and balances the rich chocolate flavor. If desired, coat the side of the frosted cake with finely shaved bittersweet chocolate, as in figures 16 and 17.*

1   **recipe Basic Chocolate Cake (*see* page 48)**
1   **recipe Coffee Buttercream (*see* page 68)**

■■ INSTRUCTIONS:

1. Prepare cake and frosting.

2. When layers are cool, frost cake.

Figure 16.
Less than an ounce of chocolate can be turned into fine shavings
to coat the side of a cake. Hold a sharp paring knife at a
45-degree angle against the flat side of a block of chocolate.
Scrape toward you, anchoring the chocolate with your other hand.

52

Figure 17.
Transfer the shavings to a plate by sliding a frosting spatula
under them. Do not pick them up with your hands, or they will
melt. To apply them, lift the shavings with the spatula and
gently touch them to the frosting. Continue until you have
covered the side of the cake.

5 3

Classic Devil's Food Cake with Whipped Cream Frosting

➤ NOTE: *This cake has more sugar than the master recipe, resulting in an extremely tender texture. It almost falls apart at the touch of a fork but turns out to be resilient and a bit spongy when chewed. The lightly sweetened whipped cream matches well with the sweeter, lighter texture of this cake. If desired, garnish with chocolate shavings (see figures 18 and 19).*

1   recipe Basic Chocolate Cake (*see* page 48), with changes below
1   recipe Whipped Cream Frosting (*see* page 83)

■■ INSTRUCTIONS:

1. Follow master recipe for Basic Chocolate Cake, making the following changes: Use two 9-by-1½-inch or -2-inch round cake pans. After dissolving cocoa and instant espresso or coffee in boiling water, stir in ¾ cup firmly packed brown sugar and ½ cup low-fat plain yogurt or buttermilk; let cool and add vanilla. Reduce butter to ½ cup (1 stick) and increase baking soda to ¾ teaspoon.

2. When layers are cool, frost cake.

Figure 18.
Thick chocolate shavings
can be used to decorate the
top of a cake. Start by
warming a block of choco-
late by sweeping a hair
dryer over it, taking care
not to melt it. Hold the
paring knife at a 45-degree
angle against the chocolate
and scrape toward you,
anchoring the block with
the other hand.

Figure 19.
Pick up the shavings with a toothpick
and place them on the cake as desired.

5 5

Old-Fashioned Chocolate Layer Cake with Chocolate Cream Frosting

➤ **N O T E :** *The milk in this cake batter slightly mutes the chocolate flavor while giving the cake a sturdy, pleasantly crumbly texture. Cream enriches the frosting, making it compatible with this less assertive chocolate cake.*

1   **recipe Basic Chocolate Cake (*see* page 48), with changes below**
1   **recipe Chocolate Cream Frosting (*see* page 79)**

I N S T R U C T I O N S :

1. Follow master recipe for Basic Chocolate Cake, making the following changes: Omit step 2 as well as boiling water. Whisk cocoa and instant espresso or coffee with flour and other dry ingredients in step 4 until no lumps of cocoa remain. Combine 1 cup plus 2 tablespoons milk at room temperature and vanilla; add alternately with dry ingredients to butter-sugar-egg mixture.

2. When layers are cool, frost cake.

Sour Cream–Fudge Layer Cake with Chocolate Butter Icing

➤ NOTE: *Sour cream gives this cake its smooth, rich chocolate flavor and dense yet melting texture, almost like fudge. An equally intense chocolate icing stands up to the rich cake. It's best not to refrigerate this cake, but if you do, cut it while cold, then let the slices come to room temperature before serving.*

1   recipe Basic Chocolate Cake (*see* page 48), with changes below
1   recipe Chocolate Butter Icing (*see* page 82)

INSTRUCTIONS:

1. Follow master recipe for Basic Chocolate Cake, making the following changes: Use two 9-by-1½-inch or -2-inch round cake pans. Increase cocoa to 1 cup. Whisk ½ cup sour cream into cocoa mixture along with vanilla. Increase butter to 1 cup (2 sticks), sugar to 1¾ cups, and baking soda to ¾ teaspoon.

2. When layers are cool, frost cake.

German Chocolate Layer Cake with Coconut-Pecan Filling

➤ **N O T E :** *Buttermilk gives this cake a pleasantly mild chocolate flavor and very light, soft texture. Be sure to divide the batter evenly between the pans (see figure 1, page 11) because these layers will rise quite high. The layers are split to create a four-tiered cake with filling covering all the layers, but with sides that are unfrosted.*

1   **recipe Basic Chocolate Cake** (*see* **page 48**), **with changes below**

1   **recipe Coconut-Pecan Filling** (*see* **page 84**)

▍ **I N S T R U C T I O N S :**

1. Follow master recipe for Basic Chocolate Cake, making the following changes: Reduce cocoa to ¼ cup and boiling water to ⅓ cup. Whisk ⅓ cup nonfat plain yogurt or buttermilk into cocoa mixture along with vanilla. Increase eggs to 3.

2. When layers are cool, halve each crosswise (*see* figures 20-24). Place one cake bottom on serving plate. Spread 1 cup filling over cake half. Place another halved cake layer over filling. Repeat this stacking and spreading process with remaining filling and cake, ending with a final layer of filling.

❧

5 8

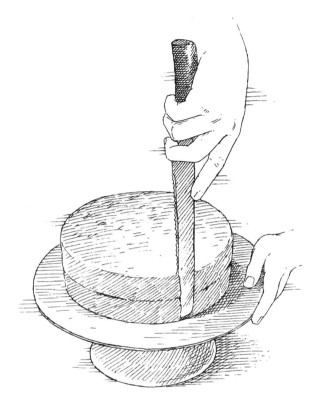

Figure 20.
For cakes with more than two layers, you will need to split each
cake layer in half. Start by making a ⅛-inch-deep cut down the
side of each cake layer with a serrated knife. This line can be used
later to align the split layers.

5 9

Figure 21.

To split the layers, place several toothpicks around the edge of the cake, halfway between the top and the bottom. Use a ruler to determine the midpoint.

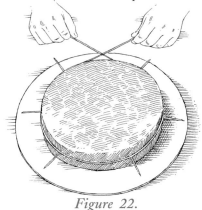

Figure 22.

Wrap a long piece of waxed dental floss around the circumference of the cake, making sure that the floss rests directly on top of the toothpicks. Cross the ends of the floss and pull. As the floss tightens, it will cut through the cake.

6 0

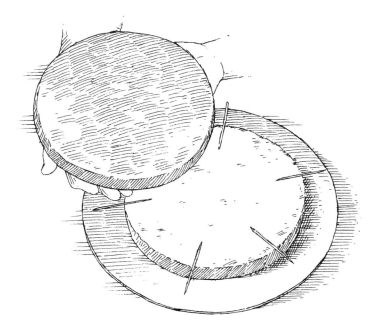

Figure 23.
Once the floss has cut through the cake, lift the top layer off and
set it aside. Remove the toothpicks from the bottom layer.

Figure 24.
Fill the cake as desired and replace the layers, realigning the
vertical cuts in the side of each layer. By putting the layers back
in their original orientation to each other, any unevenness in the
way you cut them will be concealed.

Reduced-Guilt Chocolate Layer Cake with Meringue Frosting

➤ **NOTE:** *This cake is springier than the others in this chapter and not as rich. Egg whites keep the cake soft and moist, and with less fat the chocolate flavor and color are actually more intense.*

1   recipe Basic Chocolate Cake (*see* page 48),
    with changes below

1   recipe Meringue Frosting (*see* page 80)

⠿ INSTRUCTIONS:

1. Follow master recipe for Basic Chocolate Cake, making the following changes: Whisk ½ cup vegetable oil into cocoa mixture along with vanilla. Omitting step 3, whisk 1 cup sugar with flour and other dry ingredients in step 4. Rather than mixing wet and dry ingredients in three portions as in step 4, simply add cooled cocoa mixture to dry ingredients. Beat 4 large egg whites in bowl of electric mixer at low speed until foamy. Add ¼ teaspoon cream of tartar, raise speed to medium, and beat to soft peaks. Increase mixer speed to high and beat whites until stiff and glossy. Slowly sprinkle in remaining ¼ cup sugar and beat 15 seconds more. Fold egg whites gently but thoroughly into cocoa batter. Bake only 20 to 25 minutes.

2. When layers are cool, frost cake.

chapter five

FROSTINGS AND
FILLINGS

NSWER TWO QUESTIONS BEFORE
choosing a frosting. First, how will the frosting work with the cake layers? A rich, deca-
dent chocolate ganache would overwhelm a
delicate white cake. In addition to intensity, think about the
flavors. An orange layer cake will work well with orange-
flavored frosting, but complementary pairings such as walnut
cake layers with maple meringue frosting also are possible.

The second basic question has to do with decorations. In
order to pipe rosettes or stars through a pastry bag, the
frosting must be fairly stiff and dense. Meringue frostings
and soft buttercreams are too loose. These frostings are bet-

64

ter for swirling, combing, or stippling.

This chapter begins with two basic master recipes, each with five flavor variations. One frosting is designed for optimum flavor and silkiness; the other is sturdy enough for the most elaborate designs.

The buttercream frosting (our first master recipe) has a rich, smooth texture and strong buttery flavor. The consistency is soft and supple. European buttercreams often contain six egg yolks. We like an American-style buttercream with just a few tablespoons of beaten whole egg. Made this way, the frosting tastes like butter and sugar and not eggs. However, we prefer not to omit the egg altogether. Even this small amount greatly improves the texture of the frosting and enhances the flavor of the other ingredients.

When you want to make more elaborate decorations, try our second master recipe for decorating frosting. This frosting contains more sugar, which gives it a denser, stiffer texture designed to hold its shape. We found it helpful to add a little lemon juice to cut the sweetness in this frosting.

These basic recipes are followed by a series of frostings developed for specific cakes, such as whipped cream for a yellow layer cake with strawberries or maple meringue to coat an old-fashioned buttermilk cake. Refer to the individual cake recipes in the previous chapters for suggestions on which frosting will work best.

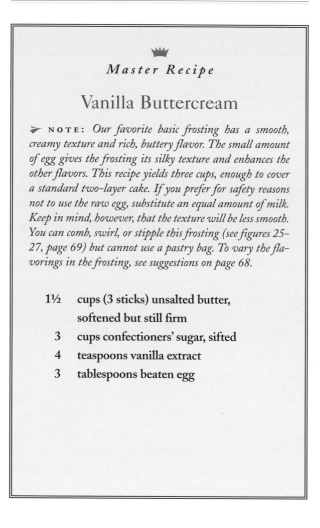

Master Recipe

Vanilla Buttercream

➤ **NOTE**: *Our favorite basic frosting has a smooth, creamy texture and rich, buttery flavor. The small amount of egg gives the frosting its silky texture and enhances the other flavors. This recipe yields three cups, enough to cover a standard two-layer cake. If you prefer for safety reasons not to use the raw egg, substitute an equal amount of milk. Keep in mind, however, that the texture will be less smooth. You can comb, swirl, or stipple this frosting (see figures 25-27, page 69) but cannot use a pastry bag. To vary the flavorings in the frosting, see suggestions on page 68.*

1½	cups (3 sticks) unsalted butter, softened but still firm
3	cups confectioners' sugar, sifted
4	teaspoons vanilla extract
3	tablespoons beaten egg

Master Instructions

1. Beat butter in bowl of electric mixer at medium-high speed until fluffy, about 1 minute. Add sugar one spoonful at a time until incorporated. Beat, scraping down sides of bowl as needed, for 3 minutes.

2. Add vanilla and egg and beat until frosting is a fluffy mass, 3 to 5 minutes. (Buttercream may be covered and kept at room temperature for several hours or refrigerated in airtight container for 1 week. Bring to room temperature before using.)

⸬ VARIATIONS:

Orange Buttercream
Follow master recipe, replacing vanilla with 3 tablespoons orange liqueur and 1½ tablespoons grated orange zest.

Lemon Buttercream
Follow master recipe, replacing vanilla with 1½ tablespoons lemon juice and 1½ tablespoons grated lemon zest.

Almond Buttercream
Follow master recipe, reducing vanilla to 1 teaspoon and adding ½ tablespoon each almond extract and almond liqueur.

Coffee Buttercream
Follow master recipe, stirring 1½ tablespoons instant espresso and 1½ tablespoons coffee liqueur into 1 tablespoon vanilla until coffee dissolves.

Chocolate Buttercream
Follow master recipe, beating in half the sugar, then adding 4 ounces melted and cooled bittersweet chocolate. Beat in remaining sugar and reduce vanilla to 1 tablespoon and beaten egg to 2 tablespoons.

Figure 25.
Once the cake is completely frosted, you may use a cake comb to
create concentric furrows on the cake top and/or sides.

69

Figure 26.
Or, use the back of a tablespoon to make decorative swirls on the
cake top and sides.

70

Figure 27.
The tip of a metal spatula may be used to stipple the top and sides of the cake.

Master Recipe

Vanilla Decorating Frosting

➤ NOTE: *This frosting contains more sugar than the Vanilla Buttercream on page 66, making it firmer and better suited to piping through a pastry bag. The lemon juice is added to help cut the sweetness. This recipe yields about four cups, enough for elaborate designs on a standard two-layer cake. See figures 28–33 (page 75) for information on how to assemble and fill a pastry bag. See chapter 6 for decorating ideas. To vary the flavorings in the frosting, see suggestions on page 74.*

1½	cups (3 sticks) unsalted butter, softened but still firm
6	cups confectioners' sugar, sifted
2½	tablespoons vanilla extract
1½	tablespoons milk
¾	teaspoon lemon juice
	Pinch salt

♛

Master Instructions

1. Beat butter in bowl of electric mixer at medium-high speed until fluffy, about 1 minute. Add remaining ingredients and beat at low speed until sugar is moistened, about 45 seconds.

2. Increase speed to medium (or high if using hand-held mixer); beat, scraping down sides of bowl as needed, until creamy and fluffy, about 1½ minutes. Avoid overbeating, or frosting will become too soft. (Frosting may be covered and kept at room temperature for several hours or refrigerated in airtight container for several days. Bring to room temperature before using.)

:: V A R I A T I O N S :

Orange Decorating Frosting

Follow master recipe, replacing vanilla and lemon juice with 4 tablespoons orange liqueur and 2 tablespoons grated orange zest.

Lemon Decorating Frosting

Follow master recipe, replacing vanilla with 2 tablespoons grated lemon zest and increasing lemon juice to 2 tablespoons.

Almond Decorating Frosting

Follow master recipe, reducing vanilla to 1½ teaspoons and adding 1 tablespoon each almond extract and almond liqueur. Omit lemon juice.

Coffee Decorating Frosting

Follow master recipe, stirring 2 tablespoons instant espresso and 2 tablespoons coffee liqueur into 1 tablespoon vanilla until coffee dissolves. Omit lemon juice.

Chocolate Decorating Frosting

Follow master recipe, reducing vanilla to 1½ tablespoons and omitting lemon juice. When frosting is fluffy, beat in 6 ounces melted and cooled bittersweet chocolate.

74

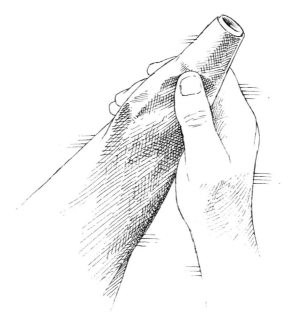

Figure 28.
A pastry bag allows for more elaborate decorations. With a new pastry bag, you may have to remove some of the pointed end to accommodate the plastic coupler. First, unscrew the ring. Insert the coupler (the cone-shaped piece of plastic), pointed end first, up into the narrow end of the pastry bag, pushing it in tightly.

75

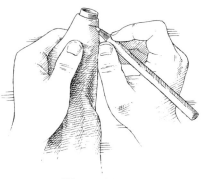

Figure 29.
With your fingernail or a pen, make a line between the first and
second groove (thread) on the coupler.

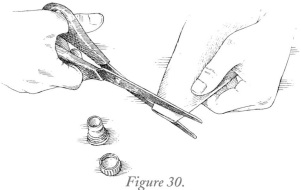

Figure 30.
Remove the coupler and cut away the bag at the mark.
Do not cut away too much of the bag, or the coupler and
icing will slip through the opening.

Figure 31.

Reinsert the coupler to expose the threads. Place a metal decorating tip over the coupler, and screw the ring tightly to secure the tip. With the coupler in place, you can change tips without having to empty the pastry bag.

Figure 32.

To fill a pastry bag, make a 3-inch cuff at the top of the pastry bag. With one hand, hold the bag open under the cuff, and with the other hand, fill the bag half full using a rubber spatula. Pack the frosting into the bag to eliminate air spaces.

77

Figure 33.
Pull the cuff back to its original position. Twist the bag just above
the icing and grip it slightly in the curve of your hand between
your thumb and forefinger. Consider this grip to be a "lock." Gentle
pressure from the other fingers of that hand squeezes the icing out of
the tip while you use your other hand to guide the bag.

Chocolate Cream Frosting

➤ NOTE: *Chocolate melted with hot cream makes a thick, rich frosting that takes well to swirling. This frosting has an intense chocolate flavor that is best suited to chocolate cakes.*

12	ounces bittersweet or semisweet chocolate, broken into pieces
1⅔	cups heavy cream
¼	cup light corn syrup

▒ INSTRUCTIONS:

1. Place chocolate in workbowl of food processor fitted with metal blade. Process until chocolate has texture of coarse sand.

2. Bring cream to boil in small saucepan. With food processor running, pour hot cream through feed tube. Add corn syrup and process just until combined.

3. Scrape frosting into bowl set over larger bowl of ice water. Stir often until frosting thickens to spreadable consistency, about 15 minutes. (Frosting can be covered and kept at room temperature for several hours or refrigerated in airtight container for several days. Bring to room temperature before using.)

Meringue Frosting

➤ **N O T E :** *A candy thermometer will guarantee the best results. Otherwise, test the syrup by dropping a small amount into a glass of ice water. When the syrup reaches 238 degrees, it should form a soft, gumlike ball in the ice water. This frosting contains no fat. The frosting does not hold up very well, however, so eat the frosted cake within a day.*

3	**large egg whites**
1	**teaspoon vanilla extract**
⅛	**teaspoon cream of tartar**
	Pinch salt
1¼	**cups sugar**

⁝ **I N S T R U C T I O N S :**

1. Beat egg whites in bowl of electric mixer at slow speed until frothy, about 1 minute. Add vanilla, cream of tartar, and salt. Beat at medium speed to soft peaks, about 1 minute. Increase to high speed and beat whites to stiff, glossy peaks, 1 to 2 minutes more. Turn off mixer.

2. Meanwhile, combine sugar and ⅓ cup water in small saucepan. Bring to boil over high heat, gently swirling pan by handle. Cover and boil 2 minutes, then carefully uncover and continue to boil until candy thermometer registers 238 degrees.

3. Return mixer to high speed and add syrup in thin, steady stream. Continue to beat, scraping down sides of bowl as needed, until frosting is cool, 7 to 10 minutes. Use immediately.

▪▪ VARIATION:

For Maple Meringue Frosting, replace sugar and water with 1¼ cups maple syrup. Place syrup in large, deep saucepan. When syrup comes to boil, reduce heat to medium, cover, and boil 2 minutes. Remove cover and boil until syrup reaches 238 degrees.

Chocolate Butter Icing

➤ NOTE: *This rich, glassy icing is designed to cover dense chocolate cakes such as Sour Cream–Fudge Layer Cake (see page 57). Choose this icing when you want a shiny, smooth finish.*

9	ounces bittersweet or semisweet chocolate
½	cup (1 stick) unsalted butter
⅓	cup light corn syrup

⁘ INSTRUCTIONS:

1. Melt chocolate and butter in medium bowl set over pan of almost-simmering water. Stir in corn syrup.

2. Set bowl over larger bowl of ice water, stirring occasionally, until frosting is just thick enough to spread, about 15 minutes. (Frosting can be covered and kept at room temperature for several hours.)

Whipped Cream Frosting

➤ **NOTE:** *In warm weather, chill the beaters and the bowl in the freezer for ten minutes before starting this recipe.*

2½   cups heavy cream, chilled
¾   cup confectioners' sugar, sifted
1   teaspoon vanilla extract

INSTRUCTIONS:

1. Beat cream in bowl of electric mixer at medium speed until thickened, about 3 minutes.

2. Add sugar and vanilla and beat, scraping down sides of bowl as needed, until stiff, about 1 minute. (Frosting can be covered and refrigerated for several hours. Briefly rewhip if necessary.)

Coconut-Pecan Filling

➤ NOTE: *This filling yields about four cups, enough to cover all four layers of the German Chocolate Layer Cake on page 58. Toast pecans in 350-degree oven for 8 minutes before chopping.*

4	large egg yolks
1	cup sugar
¼	teaspoon salt
½	cup (1 stick) unsalted butter, softened
1	cup heavy cream
1	teaspoon vanilla extract
1½	cups chopped pecans, toasted
2	cups lightly packed sweetened flaked coconut

▒ INSTRUCTIONS:

1. Mix yolks, sugar, and salt in medium bowl. Beat in butter, then gradually add cream and vanilla.

2. Pour mixture into medium nonreactive saucepan. Cook over low heat, stirring constantly, until mixture is puffy and just begins to thicken, 15 to 20 minutes.

3. Pour mixture into medium bowl and cool to room temperature. Stir in pecans and coconut. (Frosting can be covered and kept at room temperature for several hours.)

Lemon Curd Filling

➤ **NOTE:** *This thick filling is quite lemony and not terribly sweet. It will thicken as it cools.*

2	**large egg yolks**
¼	**cup sugar**
2	**tablespoons lemon juice**
1	**teaspoon grated lemon zest**
2	**tablespoons unsalted butter, softened**

INSTRUCTIONS:

1. Beat yolks and sugar in medium nonreactive saucepan until smooth. Stir in juice, zest, and butter and set pan over medium-low heat. Cook, stirring constantly, until curd thickens and becomes rich yellow color, about 3 minutes. Do not let mixture boil.

2. Pour curd through strainer. Place piece of plastic wrap directly on top of curd and refrigerate until chilled. (Lemon curd can be refrigerated in airtight container for several weeks.)

chapter six

DECORATING IDEAS

C AKE DECORATING CAN BE SIMPLE OR elaborate, depending on the amount of time you have and the desired effect. Figures 5 through 11 (*see* page 15) outline our preferred method for frosting a standard two layer cake. If using a soft buttercream, see Figures 25 through 27 (*see* page 69) for tips on combing, swirling, or stippling the frosting.

When you want a more professional look, you will need to use a decorating frosting and pastry bag. Figures 28 through 33 (*see* page 75) demonstrate how to assemble and fill a pastry bag. The illustrations in this chapter (*see* figures 34-41) offer some ideas for using a pastry bag.

A few points to remember. We find that a 14- or 16-inch nylon or polyester pastry bag is best for most uses. Advanced bakers may want a smaller bag suited to fine decorating as well.

To prolong the life of a pastry bag, wash it thoroughly in hot water after each use. If hot water is not up to the task, soak the bag in hot water splashed with a little vinegar. Air-dry the pastry bag before storing. Inverting the bag over a wine bottle can speed up this process.

Do not overfill the bag or it can be difficult to control the flow of frosting out through the tip. A bag that is two-thirds full is easy to work with.

If you are writing "Happy Birthday" or some other message on top of the cake, do this first; then apply other designs. That way, if you make a mistake, you can remove the writing, refrost the top of the cake, and try again.

When working with a pastry bag, keep a damp cloth nearby to wipe clean the opening on the decorative tip.

Figure 34.
Side swags are one of the simplest designs that can be applied
before the top border is done. Put a piece of tape across a cookie
cutter or jar lid, making sure that the edge of the tape falls
directly across the middle to create a semicircle.

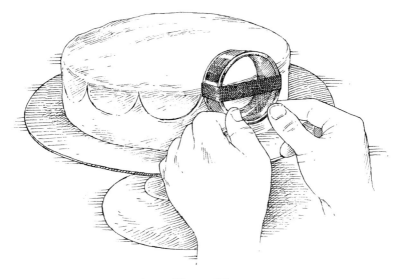

Figure 35.
Mark off sections around the cake by lining up the tape with the top edge of the cake and pressing the open semicircle into the icing.

89

Figure 36.
Pipe stars or swirls over these semicircles to create a side swag design.

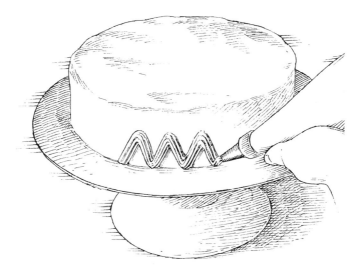

Figure 37.
To make a zigzag border, hold the pastry bag at a 45-degree
angle with the tip touching the cake's bottom edge. Using steady
pressure, move along the edge, squeezing the icing in an up-and-
down movement, being careful not to go too high. After you have
gone 3 or 4 inches, stop squeezing at the point where the tip is
near the platter and partially rotate the cake stand. Repeat this
process until you have gone completely around the cake and
joined the last stroke to the first.

Figure 38.
To give a cake a finished look, add borders to the top and/or bot-
tom edge. To make a shell border, hold the pastry bag at a 45-
degree angle. Using medium pressure, squeeze out a puff of icing.
As you move to the right, lessen your pressure on the bag to make
a "tail." Stop the pressure and lift up the tip.

Figure 39.
Make another puff, overlapping it onto the end of the first tail,
and again move to the right and release the pressure to create
another tail. Repeat this process to create a shell border all the
way around the cake.

Figure 40.
Rosettes and stars may be used to make a border or decorate the top of a cake. Both shapes are made with the pastry bag at a sharp angle. When repeating either shape, space each new one so that it touches the previous one. Rosettes are made by squeezing out a tiny circle of icing, never changing the angle at which the bag is held.

Figure 41.
Stars are made by squeezing out a bit of icing, letting up on the pressure, then immediately lifting the tip.

93

index

9 4